Slugs and Snails

CLAIRE LLEWELLYN • BARRIE WATTS

W
FRANKLIN WATTS
LONDON•SYDNEY

First published in 2001 by Franklin Watts,
96 Leonard Street, London EC2A 4XD

Franklin Watts Australia
14 Mars Rd
Lane Cove
NSW 2066

Series editor: Anderley Moore
Editor: Rosalind Beckman
Series designer: Jason Anscomb
Designer: Joelle Wheelwright
Illustrator: David Burroughs

A CIP catalogue record is available
from the British Library.

ISBN 0 7496 3690 4

Dewey Classification 595.78

Printed in Hong Kong/China

Contents

What are slugs and snails?

Slugs and snails belong to a large family of animals called molluscs.

A mollusc is a creature with a soft, slimy body, which is often protected by a shell.

Slugs and snails are very alike. The big difference between them is that snails have shells and slugs do not.

More than half of all slugs and snails live in the sea. The others live in freshwater rivers and ponds, or in shady places on land.

Compare the size of the garden snail (top) with its huge African relation.

There are over 60,000 different kinds of slugs and snails. Some of them are too small to see; others are as long as your arm.

◀ *Most slugs are not very pretty, but some are colourful like this sea slug from Florida.*

Where they live

Slugs and snails live in many places. You will often find them in woods where there is always food and shelter.

Grove snails are able to cling to rocky hillsides or steep cliffs.
▼

▲ *You will also find slugs in grassy meadows.*

▲ *The great pond snail lives at the bottom of ponds.*

Slugs and snails are easy to find in gardens and parks. They come out when it is cool – in the early morning, evening or at night – or after a shower of rain. During the day, they hide in damp places, under trees and bushes, among fallen leaves or under piles of rocks or rubbish.

Slugs have no shells so they can squeeze their way under loose bark or burrow into the ground.

▲

In the daytime, snails rest against walls and fences or hide in pots and under stones.

The body

Slugs and snails have very similar bodies. The soft, rubbery part is called the foot. It is covered with a sticky coat of slime. This helps the animal to move, and to cling on to windows and walls.

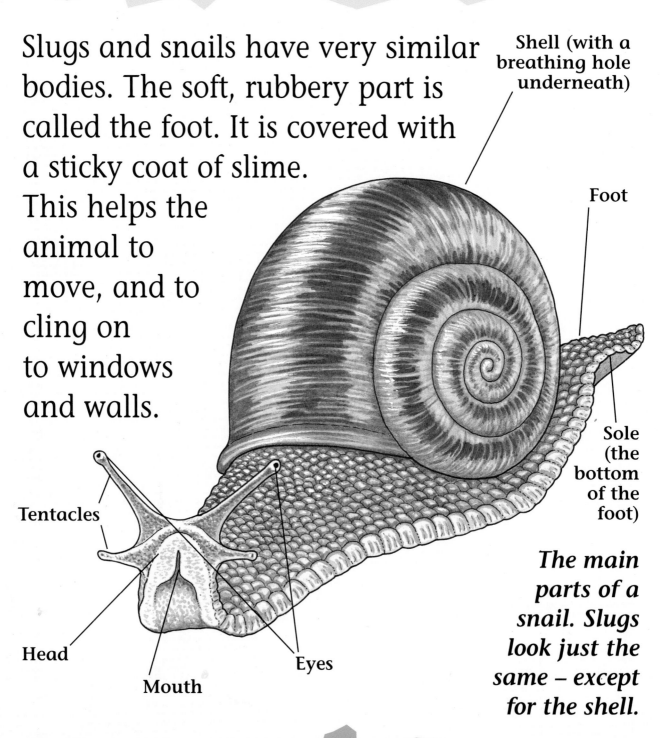

Shell (with a breathing hole underneath)

Foot

Sole (the bottom of the foot)

Tentacles

Head

Mouth

Eyes

The main parts of a snail. Slugs look just the same – except for the shell.

The mantle is a thick fold of skin on top of the foot. It contains a small breathing hole that can open and close. In snails, the mantle helps to make the shell.

A close-up of a slug's mantle, showing the breathing hole.

Both creatures have two pairs of tentacles on their heads. At the end of the longer pair are tiny eyes. The shorter pair pick up smells and tastes.

Moving along

Slugs and snails move by swimming along on a smooth layer of slime. This makes it much easier to move on rough ground. The slime also protects the sole of the foot and stops it from getting torn.

▲ *The silvery trails left behind by snails and slugs show where they have been.*

Slugs and snails leave silver trails behind them. You can often see these in the morning, before they have dried up and disappeared.

Slugs and snails creep along on the sole of their foot. Muscles in the foot ripple forwards in waves, lifting each part of the body in turn, so that the animal glides forwards.

A slug leaves its trail on a leaf.

The sole of a snail's foot.

Most snails move at about 10 metres an hour. At that rate, it would take a snail six years to travel non-stop from London to Edinburgh!

A snail's shell

A snail builds its own shell, and as the snail gets older so its shell grows bigger. New layers of shell are made by the mantle and added to the bottom of the shell. The new shell is thin and brittle at first but quickly hardens.

As it grows bigger, the shell curls round in a spiral called a whorl.

Snail shells can be tall and narrow, or short and wide. They can be smooth and glossy, or dull and rough. Most shells have coloured flecks or stripes, but some are completely plain.

A snail can pull its whole foot inside its shell. This protects it from an enemy. It also keeps its body moist when the weather is cold or very dry.

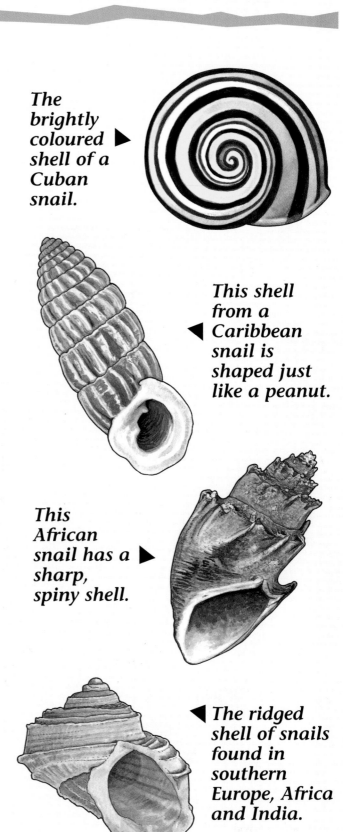

The brightly coloured shell of a Cuban snail.

This shell from a Caribbean snail is shaped just like a peanut.

This African snail has a sharp, spiny shell.

The ridged shell of snails found in southern Europe, Africa and India.

Feeding

Most slugs and snails feed on animal droppings, fungi and dead and rotting animals and plants. The animals eat by rubbing their food with a long, narrow tongue called a radula.

The radula works like a cheese grater. It is covered with rows of tiny teeth that shred the solid food.

The tip of the radula is always wearing out and breaking off. This doesn't matter because the other end never stops growing.

A few slugs and snails are pests in gardens and on farms. They chew holes in green plants and can destroy young seedlings. They eat soft berries and other fruit, or spoil it with their slime.

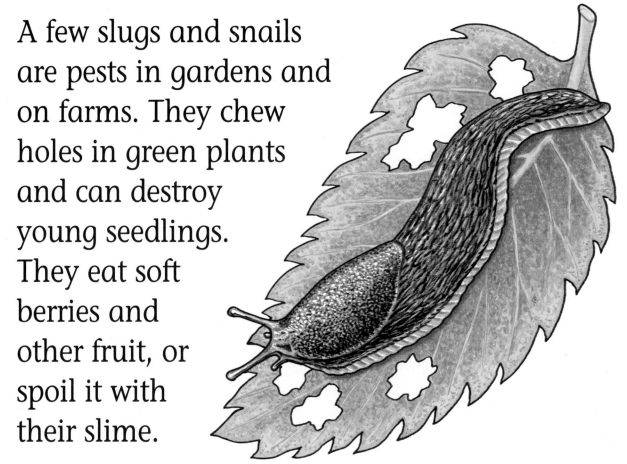

Slugs destroy plants by chewing holes in them.

Mating

Slugs and snails do not have to mate to have young. Most of them have both male and female parts to their body, and can make and lay eggs on their own. But most of them prefer to find a mate.

Slugs and snails usually mate in the summer. The two animals make a lot of slime and then lie very close to one another.
▼

A few weeks after mating, both animals lay their eggs. Eggs are laid mostly in the summer and autumn. In autumn there is less danger of the eggs drying up.

Slugs and snails lay 20–100 eggs. The eggs lie hidden in the soil, among dead leaves or under logs and stones.

▲
The eggs look like tiny balls. Some are soft and clear; others have a chalky white shell.

Growing up

Slug and snail eggs hatch in batches. The first batch may hatch in three weeks; then another batch hatches a month or two later, and so on. Sometimes a whole batch of hatchlings are eaten by predators or killed by dry weather. Spreading the hatching in batches gives the young a better chance to survive.

▲

These eggs are ready to hatch, but most slug or snail eggs never reach this stage.

The newly-hatched slugs and snails look just like their parents. They grow quickly as they feed. Most kinds are fully grown by the end of a year, but the largest take up to four years.

Many slugs and snails die before they are able to lay eggs of their own. Only five eggs in 100 will survive to become an adult.

Some slugs and snails live for 50 years, but most of them have much shorter lives and end up as meals for other animals.

▲
A newly-hatched snail.

Enemies

Slugs have many enemies. They are eaten by hedgehogs, shrews, frogs, toads, slow-worms and some fierce beetles. All these animals are the gardener's friends because they cut down the number of slugs.

A frog enjoys its meal of slugs.

Many snails are eaten by birds. A snail may tuck itself up in its shell, but some birds have learned to break the shell and get at the snail inside.

A blackbird can easily smash a shell with its beak.
▼

The song thrush uses a stone to break the shell. It will use the same stone over and over again.
▼

Birds do not like a snail's sticky slime because it gums up their beak. They always wipe the body on the ground before eating it.

A long rest

In winter, snails and slugs take a long rest. This is called hibernation. They do this because the plants they depend on for food and shelter die back in the cold weather.

Snails often hibernate in clusters. They become active in the spring when the air begins to warm.

▼

In some parts of the world, snails take a summer sleep to survive long spells of hot, dry weather. Some of the larger snails in California have slept for eight whole years!

To protect themselves in winter, snails tuck their foot up inside their shell and seal the door with slime. The slime soon dries as hard as leather, and stops water escaping from the animal's body.

▲
A sealed snail shell.

◀ *Slugs burrow into the soil or under logs or stones during the winter.*

Snail & slug surprises

Most water snails take in oxygen from the water, but some come up to the surface and breathe in the air.

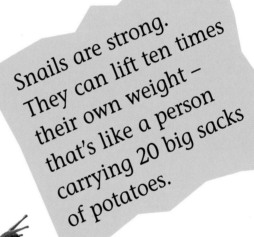

Snails are strong. They can lift ten times their own weight – that's like a person carrying 20 big sacks of potatoes.

Some people enjoy eating snails cooked with butter and garlic. They use a special fork to get the snail out of the shell.

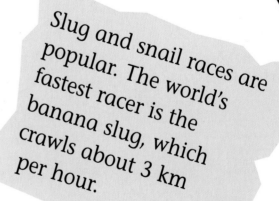

Slug and snail races are popular. The world's fastest racer is the banana slug, which crawls about 3 km per hour.

A snail from Brazil has the world's longest shell. It's 10 cm long – about twice as long as your thumb.

In 1846, a 'dead' desert snail that had spent four years glued to a display board in the Natural History Museum in London woke up and began to feed. It lived for another two years.

The largest snail is the African giant snail. It measures up to 39 cm – that's about as long as your arm. The giant snail weighs just under 1 kg – about the same as a big bag of sugar.

Most garden snails live for 2–3 years. You can keep track of them by numbering their shells with a pen.

Glossary

Foot	The soft, rubbery part of a slug or snail's body.
Hibernation	A long winter sleep that helps animals survive in cold weather.
Mantle	The thick fold of skin on a slug or snail's body.
Mollusc	A family of animals with soft, slimy bodies, that are often protected by shells. Snails and slugs are kinds of mollusc.
Muscle	A part of an animal's body that helps it to move.
Radula	The grater-like tongue of a slug or snail.
Sole	The bottom of a slug or snail's foot.
Tentacle	One of the four horns on a slug or snail's head.
Whorl	The shape of the coils in a snail's shell.

Index